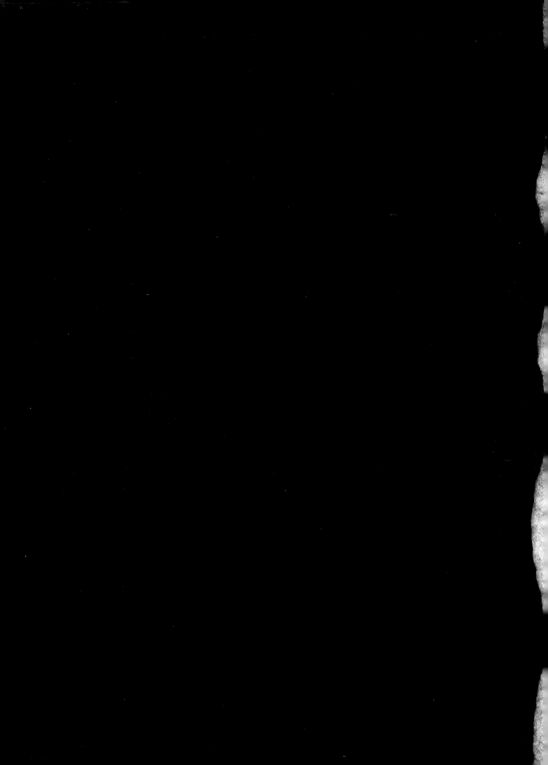

# Nightly, at
# the Institute
# of the Possible

*D M Gordon*

"Voix du Sang" used with permission
of the estate René Magritte

Printed and published by
Hedgerow Books/Levellers Press
Amherst & Florence, Massachusetts

ISBN  978-0-9819820-6-9

*To you, much loved, who h*
*life and clarity to these*

# CONTENTS

## I

## II

## III

IV

V

I

# RAVEN

First on the road, stripping flesh,
then on my shoulder, squeezing,
miniature and blind, it appeared
when I was young, uniformed,
and driven to Saint Sebastian's School.

With me most days, it smells life.
I find small digs in my skin,
and sometimes feathers brush my ear.
Outside chapel, black birds find each other,
form cities, raise generations of shadows
while I squirm on the worn bench.

At night the wind comes through the sashes,
makes my dry house sing against its will;
my shutters shake like weak elbows.
It's then, tiny enough to fit in my pillbox,
the raven sleeps.

I would give this small pinching thing to you,
then smoke salmon caught
from the river as it left the sea.
Hang the shining flesh over green wood,
so together, you, and I, and the raven
could eat the body of the old soul that swam so far,
then the roe, its tiny stars, its possibilities.

## ABOUT A DECOY

—about its greeting to those who exploded
before its painted eyes; how it couldn't feel sudden chill,
oblivious, almost, to the splashings of the hunter's dog,
righting itself soon after.

                                Still it was made from living things,
and swelled on wet days till its lacquer crazed
in wrinkles like my own. In dry September,
it was dual-natured, belly freighted with water,
yet blistered, splitting in a crevice along its spine.
Drakes, drawn from their work in the sky, spooked
at the ruptured wood—then settled beside it.

Now this decoy, in the great room of my inn, placed
on mirrored glass, lends its life to the lie of home,
these quiet steps, this polished wood.

# PRAYER

The old horse in my barn,
                not fearing lightning,
licks his bowl clean of molasses. He and I
are gray with trees and sky.
                In the red light
of a holy place nearby, men in white cassocks
lie face down,
                crucified, candlelit and alive,
whips in their hands, loving God.
The world cannot hold us much longer,
virus that we are,
                crackling down the wires
we have strung for ourselves.
                A hurricane is coming.
Rain will become a different thing.
The old horse sheds his winter coat.
                Unable to change the past,
I find myself hammering for happiness,
wishing to become unhistorical, praying
for a transfer of equine innocence,
thick-lipped and thoughtless as grass.

# MEDICINE

For demonic possession, release the dragons—
iridescent, white to fight the unnamed,
salmon-colored to attack the known.
Imagine these, full grown with folded wings,
small enough to fit inside an embryonic cell,
sent after demons, equally ancient, equally small,
who show themselves the way creatures in opaque ponds
create concentric rings unseen, break the skin
and return to hide in the mud—corkscrewed worms,
unbound by tissue, blood or bone.
The war proceeds between the winged and wingless,
and as in all histories, the winner will write it—
the winning will be deemed good. Though every demon,
electric, toxic, feels it is a child of the universe,
yet isn't there something always wrong about invasion,
something always noble about defense?
So, the end of the story; a figure on a lacquered bridge
over swollen runoff, a churning pond behind,
a losing army. It's April, ice on all the edges,
the air hurts wonderfully to breathe.
The water foams white. The sky, late and high,
is riddled with salmon-colored contrails—

# NOCTURNE

Rest your head on my breast.
Something in the woods is after the cats.
Ansel, soft and warm with sun, is gone.
Adam, seduced by the glitter of leaves,
never came back. Shut your eyes
while my voice hums, as the weight
of your hidden world pins me,
as we listen to our last cat lap rain on the balcony.
We can try to believe in the verdict of leaves,
try to drift, and wake to fog-piercing
trees waiting to burn bright.

# DENYING ARCHEOLOGY

Strange to think of peas as old,
older than tubers, or pale carrots,
to think of fingers, sex unknown, nail-bitten,
snatching the first found pod,
upping the pace in a rush of sweet,
the tasted flowers, then the leaves,
till the vine emptied. How long
before restraint allowed the pea
to dry in woven sacks? How long
before soup sprinkled with sage,
before stacked tins, before freezer doors
breathing clouds on waxed boxes in the market?
And I, relying on the farmer,
the weaver, electrician and truck driver,
and this year, planting for myself,
have learned nothing, but hungry
this morning in the yard,
spring-fevered and sugar low,
I ate the sweet thin pods, every last one,
long before they could grow old.

# GUEST

It's an ancient ritual—*xenia*;
sweets and savories, a bottle of wine
and no questions asked of the stranger
who, full-bellied now, yells *fuck you*
in the driveway, practicing his backhand
against the garage with deadly strength.
His car is broken down in the cul-de-sac.
Waiting for a tow, he hits a ball
through the window and bombs the guppy bowl.
We hide the bodies from the children.
We've been polite, carefully curious,
struggling with the stench, the foolish
intelligence and wild balls, because
one never knows if the idiot in the yard
kicking up the leaves and confiding in the cat,
might be the original god package.

## ABOUT LYING

Abandoning the slide on a tin hot day,
I said, *I have a horse.*

I lied to make it true.
A mare with spangled mane.

As I spoke, she blew into my hair
and grazed, innocent of my love and fear
in the green dark shade.

So I understand Superman
and, maybe, even heaven;

in the beginning I imagine
God, tired of longing, said:
*I have a firmament*
*A horse*
*A man*

# RESEARCH

They had wings but lost them,
making them less than ideal.

When we chopped away appendages
they still soared, coasting to controlled landings
even after removal of their abdomens.

They retained a strange interest
in staying near their home.

When we covered their eyes
with dots of polish, they sank.

We hung fabric rainbow
high in the forest, then dropped them
by the hundreds, and they veered
acutely towards the light.


*after Elizabeth Svoboda, New York Times, April 4, 2006*

# ZERO

—a mark forced to swallow its tail, excluding
what's beyond the pale for what's inside.

Poles tacked with wire perfectly circle the garden
to keep the fawns away; zero fawns–
but strawberries.
                    The concept *one*
seems less dilemma;  singular, easy to identify;
one flat-pawed mole peeking out its tunnel
nibbling strawberries. One mole.
                              One heart of mole
beating many times a second, the many hours
of one molish life.
                    If the problem of zero is purity,
the problem of one is plural because one becomes
a he or she, a sow or bull. One implies an other, then all
the tiny mole hearts pumping on patches of turf
claimed from savanna to tundra, all that living,
all that dying in the Hades of crabgrass now,
in the seconds it takes to think this, the opposite of zero,
                    the poisoned, the old, the million
wiggling pups, each smaller than a word, licked clean
and nursing at the nipples of its mole mother.

And what does the sow feel,
as she scoops her pups to breast with perfect mitts,
for I don't doubt the sow's heart, fierce and puzzled
as my own after birthing, her passion
or my own, not singular, not empty, not bowing
to logic or anything to do with zero;
even in plain emptiness, unseen electrons yearn.


*after Susan Stewart*

II

## SEA TURTLE

Older than Venus,
not big-breasted with flesh-folded hips
and fashioned to stand in an altar,
the turtle consumes and weeps our taint,
in tears that fall for miles through light-starved sea
to waiting albino worms. It comes in dream if it comes at all,
rising through the murk to say

> *Drape your tired body over me; I will take you*
> *to where air begins its desire,*
> *to the seeds of what you've known*
> *and what you have forgotten.*

# SOUTANE

Trying not to think of God thumping down
in snow clumps blown from pin oaks,
of twig shadows on snow—like leaded glass,
blank spaces where the saints have departed—
spinning his soutane round his ankles,
watched by a black bird, the wool shagged
with ice, his black slippers sparking the winter sun,
trying not to think of God skittering like
dried leaves over marshmallow ice,
he thinks of the espresso Maria served at dawn
in small pinched cups, his own raw fingers,
how they cranked the ice cream freezer at Aunt Sally's,
how he could taste, even now,
the vanilla and salt on his lips. Trying to feel
the wind razor his cheeks, drunk on blood, wishing away
the lanced side and everything he'd ever been taught
for the frost biting his toes and his shifting balance,
he craves this kiss of anything that could make God small.

## ON THE ROGUE RIVER

When I walked down the path at dusk
from the home I built on the edge of the cliff,
I took care not to step on the snails.
They littered the way, absorbed with each other.
I picked my way through them
to where my friends danced
in their tin-roofed cabin under the cliff,
the music thinned by the roar of the water.
We danced until our skin was wet,
clothes crumpled in a wicker chair,
ran steaming into the black river
while night birds sailed back to my house.
With closed-eyed fever we danced, held
by blank windows, while behind the music
the face crumbled, the godlike face of the cliff.
The snails turned toward the river,
the water-not-stone of the river.
We whirled till our feet refused,
curled to sleep while day met night,
sweeping away on cedar rafts,
a scattered flotilla of snails.

# FREE RADICAL

It's not the traffic, a hot river slowed
on I-91; it's the loose dog—
not that he's loveable with his trashcan head.
Look, I say to the fairy,
smudged lipstick, mascara and a wand.
On the seat between us, a pumpkin
with Magic Marker eyes.
The dog scoots among stopped cars.
There's a party atmosphere, children waving
through passenger windows, the sky crayon blue.
Police try to catch the dog.
When we come to be in front, he is calm.
It isn't the officer un-holstering
his gun. It isn't the dog's heart blossoming
on a stalk of blood, or the spread legs of the man,
shot after shot, or the smile that escapes him
as he houses his gun and waves us on.
It's the stillness of the wand.

# SHADOW, SCENT AND WARMTH

She watches as a spaceship, like a Ferris wheel,
skims over jeweled lawn; scarlet metal docking
at the second floor of the barn.
The double doors used to take in hay;
now, muscle girls swing gaffs and hawsers,
and beyond, a time-trussed corridor leads
to lost smells of cows and chicken dust,
the moans of obsolete conveyer belts.
*A person could survive on this,*
she says to the stranger next to her—
a man of shadow, scent, and warmth.
They watch the wheel settle in its berth.
*We could escape,* she says.
But seduced by his rumors of resilient fields,
she folds into his arms,
nightly, at the Institute of the Possible.

# ENCORE

When Archie reached for the girl
in the pink poodle skirt, the sleeve
of his letter sweater caught on the straws
and shot them into the air,
tiny rockets of his heart
that she stepped on when she danced.

He switched too soon from root beer
to boilermakers, barflies watching
the tiny vessels of his cheeks blossom
as, the girl long gone,
he repeated his loneliness.

Disinterred in 2294, a late Petroleum Age
specimen, the fossils of his memory, read
by a research assistant with a handheld MRI,
showed disentangled love-knots of blame
in rivers of gin. The assistant noted
contours of a mother's breast and
a poodle skirt. Not another one,
she sighed, and moved on.

# DIFFERENT GOLD THAN GILT

1.

In the forest pigs snuff truffles,
white for cream sauce, black for shadows.
And after, tied with bibs
for the annual employees banquet,
they taste millet and toast as unique—
separate from pumpkin—a revelation
when, for 364 days, all they've had is slops.
They're on their best behavior, powdered
and bathed, touching cloven toes together
the way schoolgirls cross white-socked ankles.
They're served a truffle
on arugula, spindled with oil,
      enough to break their hearts,
      the way we buy tickets for the lottery.

2.

A dog lifts his leg on alyssum at Versailles,
a different gold than gilt. You have a fuzzy notion
of his past life as Van Gogh. It's the yellow.
You notice he has one torn ear and smile
to yourself, but he catches you and leers.
He's ambitious, on his way across the continent
from patch to patch of white tufty flowers, covering
their perfume with his more important smell,
taking control of all the world, a small brindled Bonaparte.
He corrects for past mistakes, thinks in horizons
instead of maps. At the first great port he may stow away,
or not—he's a mongrel after all, and hell may have
choices—

       might start again in Brazil, where the scent
       of white has changed, but is still other.

3.

While biologists take notes in Land Rovers,
elephant matriarchs discuss social solutions
with rumbles as inaudible as the sound of dry
ground. What if elephants are as chatty
as a stomach you lay your ear against?
What if trees talk all the time, and we don't
have the right stethoscope? In my back yard
a salt and pepper rabbit clacks her teeth.
Snails embrace with attention
that puts Siddhartha's concubines to shame.
And in a puddle on the road, National Public Radio
is recording microbes, who chatter like a claque
        before the opera, primed to clap after every aria;
        have you heard the microbes sing?

# HORSES ARE NOT PREDATORS

Most moments they're aware, wordless
in their flesh, sleep is dangerous.
When they must, they lie briefly on the sand,
aberrant, misshapen mounds.
They see two planes at once,
the horizon and crushed grass—
a landscape without vanishing points.
One eye doesn't tell the other what it knows,
one frightened, the other consoled.
Two eyes won't say if yellow is a lion
or a wild receipt windblown from a truck.
Smart ones never linger to find out.
The weight of heart and hide falls to teacup joints
lotteried to shatter; they are mindful
to keep other flanks near for wolves to find.
Herdless life is netless; friendship lulls like prayer.
You and I are predators, busy with defining.
We sleep for hours, then sleep haunts us
when we wake, while horses we've observed
swish flies in dusty paddocks, half asleep.

III

# WAITING

He wishes he were in a hammock again
where he followed her into the tropics,
with courage to light a match
at the small yellow death crawling
in the sand. She is the river loosened,
decades of insisting everything sing along,
and it does, men in blizzards, scorpions,
and beasts who grind.their teeth. She grasps
the humming trees as easily as electricity,
carries the fragrance of cactus, memories
of warm mud and the grizzly who frightened
their pack horses. She hangs a mist-green scarf
to dry on the hook of a crescent moon
and he could see it up there just after dawn
if she slept late, but she never does.
She is the water he tries to keep in his fingers,
and far away now, she is finding her way
back to this hill which steams through snow.
He is not a river, but finite and breakable
as this white cup with which he waits for her.

# LIVING TREASURE

*(Japanese Cup)*


If she were a cup he fashioned, conceived
in every curve with longing, waiting
under his table in the shed—patient
in the slip-pail while cast off sketches fell,
fighting dry time, his fingers white
with her wet skin, he wouldn't dream
of breasts, but cavities with steaming tea,
he would dream translucence, her arm pressed
to earthy hips, every flaw adored,
he'd dream her heart set in wood-fire, fixed
as he made her, with curious imperfections.

# ABOUT ARGUMENT

What slipped between them,
skittered smooth as soap
and into the past, irretrievable,
slump-shouldered,
scratched with what will become memory.

That night as he slept, she read
the braille crepe of his eyelids,
the scent of distress on her fingertips.

 In his dream, the wedge of her
carelessness hissed in a lavender river
into which (he will tell her in the morning,)
she released a tiny red boat.

# PERFECT PITCH

Blackbird cocks, little carnies
on the midway in the marsh, calling
*Take Me* (I know you—waiting
at the wood's edge, quick-eyed and still)
*Take Me* (I'm the consummation
of all red-shouldered blackbirds
who've ever seen the sun)
*Take Me* (There's only one worthy passion
and it shakes this clawful of grass)

Oh, the dimes I've thrown at milk bottles
trying to win the big blue dog

# STALLS

Warm clouds forced from aching
nostrils, hunger, trampled straw, muzzles
raked across bars. Riago cranes
his long neck to rest his jaw
over the partition, touching noses
with Regent who rattles his bucket,
whose breath and agitation are familiar,
but whose eye Riago can't see,
the touching uncomfortable,
the craving unrelieved.
He knows Rasta's smell, the opening
vagina and sudden sweet urine,
and she knows the grinding of his jaws,
the sound of his falling body,
as I know yours in tangled sheets,
your breath harsh from cigarettes,
sighing thoughts I can't read,
wine I refused tonight.
I'm here, and unable to stay,
falling to the warming dark. Under
the pillow my fingers find the tips of yours,
your eyes already closed, my eyes closing,
the stretch to touch effortless,
the habit as thick as stall walls.

# CELLO IN APARTMENT 2B

Waiting where he perched her
in a corner, silent, absorbing
smells of garlic beef, his only specialty,
shrinking from the room's heat,
she's been with many thighs—with his,
cradled naked, moonless nights;
and left by many thighs—by his,
stood to face the flash of other hips,
a rising foot, painted toes, the coos
of his tattooed other-shes, all who leave
eventually. After each abandonment, he strokes
the spider crinkles of her face. *Old Girl*
he calls her, and makes her moan—
hugs her as she presses his thighs, bites his fingers
till he laughs and shakes them burning in the air.
He will draw the bow on a courante,
play in fourth position, her arched back
against his chest, her G string rubbed
by taut bleached hair, his head back,
their necks exposed; her spruce ribs
hum between his knees, now swaying
in the rhythm of the slip and slide,
now tightening at the radiator's hiss.

# POTATO CANNONS

Her boys stand outside the sagging barbed wire
in this time before dusk; the cow keeps an eye
on her calf. With white and shining tubes,
they take aim over the field, imagining themselves
heroes in alleys, steel barrels poked at hip's height.
They fill their chambers with AquaNet,
that relic from a time when women
forced themselves into girdles
and hairspray was their battle helmet,
the sticky gas trapped to spark ejections
aimed two-handed at the pear tree and horizon.
Potatoes hurl with a whoosh any philandering
god would envy and the calf tears from the nipple,
scooting towards the shed. Which shattered spud
will keep an eye intact and sprout?
Behind the kitchen window, arms wrapped
around a bowl filled with greens, she watches
the postures of the boys, their lengthening silhouette.

## TO MY MOTHER IN HER SORROW ON OUR TWENTIETH ANNIVERSARY

I am the one who was never born.
Say holy to darkness, our history
of hours un-erasable.

      When you escaped me,
I was, I am, the one content not to have lived.

The peach remembers rain by its mold,
wasps with its sap.

      Broods wind fallen.
Says holy to darkness.

       Would you have gone
in my place?

    Listen.

      I am not the grass or heat,
or age, or sorrow, but midwinter without longing.
Say holy to darkness, our small histories.

The fruit completes under the tree,
in burning shade which creeps in living things,
as we unborn begin in dimness, creasing and folding,
already maps.

Release me, and do not cry.

      Gone in my place,
      every child of the world.

# LAST RITES

The first long night he left
      an apple on her table.
Morning came. He brought
      lime ice to her lips.
He brought tiny chocolate mice
      with silver tails and
      traces of sage to which she clung.
A fly rode her confused, sensuous hand.
Outside her window, a white-gloved ocean.

What I mean by ocean is omniscience.
What I mean by sensuous is perfect.
Sage is the scent of wild hills.
Tiny mice with silver tails, adoration.
The apple, an apology for desire.

## MONTANA TRUCKS

Near the bull thistle closest to the sun
and looking down, down to the dry stream bed,
to the truck left standing on its grill as if a child
put it there, it being August, when the badgers
own it all and the quail-hen schools her chicks
in the slow motioned Church of Invisibility,
she stares with folded arms. The truck has been
there long enough to look shot full of holes,
like the other trucks, the ghost green Chevy
in the next ravine, puffy bench seats eaten by squirrels,
the silver Dodge from Deer Lodge,
paintless frames in the Crazies, in the Big Belts,
in the Bitterroot. She thinks about the cowless cowboy
who drove this one, ears popping, to this high curve—
it must have been in summer, because snow is deep here
until June—1963 Montana plates tumbling, headlights
over rear guard, and she knows the cowboy didn't use a seat belt.
Cowboys believe in freedom. She'd like to think
he walked away, a blood blossom on his pearly buttoned shirt,
a badge of honor. She'd like to think the stars were out,
a moon for him as he pulled himself by sapling tips
to where she stands, that he came back as witness,
showed sons and daughters who had sons and daughters—
and that they'll walk away too. When the bars close
from Butte to Lame Deer, they'll be here.

The badger, feisty as he is, won't chase them off
the mountain, and the quail chicks, what's left of them,
will be on the move nearby, slow and visible.

# READING ABOUT THE DOG

who might dream in smells
might read the scent of birdsong
she is told to forget what she knows

*toes*
*smell puzzled*

It's all in how dogs receive her love
in how their torsos fit her human arms
their willful click-clacking shadows

The vestige of a complex god
survives in their nose
If she dismisses dog-love as instinct
she might dismiss her own

*time*
*is fading scent*

She can't read their post-its
on the white board of her lawn

*whiffs*
*of sarcasm*

When her dog, who likes her cooking
veers off trail into undergrowth,
she hears a cry, and parts the ferns
to find him bloodied in the bowels of a fawn

*Taste*
*of completion*

She whips him with willow
to loosen his bite
and hurls him into the river
to cure him of his DNA

He swims upstream and back to her
as innocent of her as she is of him
addicted as she is to his happiness

# ARROW

—a penciled line on paper dropped here
at her feet where she's come to catch a train.

She stares at letters, sans serif and senseless
on the page, and under them, the arrow drawn.

She's going to a place she's never been
where her mother has retired to newly reclaimed desert;

she was leaving on track four but the arrow points
to ten, and just now, while she was distracted,
a gritty shoe left its print and twisted it to exit.

She abandons plans to visit her mother
whom she blames for everything.

She might take a ticket to Odessa because
it's in the novel she is reading, though
nothing good occurred in that chapter.

There's music in the name, Odessa—Texas
or Ukraine. Arrow. There is white space.

Odessa on the Black Sea sixteen hundred years ago,
colonized by travelers like herself. She has seen
denuded hills of Scotland, what it took to cobble
all the wooden ships squeaking at their berths.

A man with a creel of snow crab gives her
a baited line, and fog comes in. The line becomes

a penciled line on paper dropped on concrete.
This is what she has, an arrow and the world.

# AGAINST THE BIT

*for Amy*


But you've been almost dead for days,
love, pulling water halfway up a straw,
sweet to the hallucinated dog.
The bed sheets cut like swords.
You sit up to eat corn flakes
with the last slippery spoon.
We focus on the bowl—plastic, scratched,
a blue field of dancing lambs—
as if it held more kitchen mornings,
as if you'll escape brass handles waiting.
Ready with the paring knife, I ask
if you'd like a little more banana.
A drop of milk on your lips. In your eyes,
my reflection crowded out.

I would drag you to the carousel to ride,
to the glass house lit at dusk over the ocean,
where each horse is open mouthed against the bit,
where there are endless easy golden rings,
and the music is thick as a cage.

# HOW LIKE WINGS

Flying at the bottom of the pool
Chlorine blue overhead
Slice, reach and pull
       strong as a bird of paradise
Leaving behind without desire
      other swimmers
      the man outside the chain link fence

No one speaks    Calm
The day-sky blankets them
How long does she crouch underwater
Seeing nothing
          Not answering questions
Sun-dappled, pavonine, her eyes sting
How like wings untrapped hair
      trying to swim away

Useless to cry under water
She breaks the easy ceiling to find
An uncompassed race against age
Herself at the lapping edge

## OLD MIRROR

He proposed making love
in the most conventional place, a carved pew,
his slow invasion. And if she'd declined,
would he have forced the sea walls down?
His night wind rustled tiny orchids,
broke the demitasse on her window ledge
and blew his rose curtain of rain across
her naked hips, and after, she dreamed
she must hurry to bury a body dismembered
by someone's violence. When the generations
failed her, he was there. When he stopped
touching her, she loved him most.

She still keeps a remnant of him,
a piece of ocean in her pocket, like an old mirror
wrapped in a sock, reminding her how once
he rose from surf all in a seal's eye. Now
she has no word for god strong enough to carry her.

# THE FIRST LAW OF
# THERMODYNAMICS

Does she feel better now?
Words she launched into the field are tangled
balls of temper, which dazed a cricket, who stopped
mid-chirp, then caught his ankles in their tendrils.
She knows they're still out there by the silence.

Energy transformed but not created
or destroyed; the ancient streamers
of her tricycle now translucent shards, the blue
molecules rained into the ravine of her childhood.

She listens for the cricket to restart, to signal
that the field has begun to decompose her pique.
But what if her words have stirred the rivalries
of field mice? What if they condense, transform,

become a tick which jumps on to her cuff
and she wastes three gallons to flush it away,
the little swimming legs of what once was unkindness
spiraling down and out of sight, but not out of existence.

## ISLANDS IN THE GULF

What fog erased and built again—
warm plums and cormorants,
bark peel and pale flesh scarred with initials,
adult laughter, running away.

We clung to cliffs like seabirds,
over water, octopus deep,
grabbed green tickets for passage through trees,
free in our prison
because we were small.

Here, a man built a castle,
a tower for himself and one for his wife,
empty now, the smell of box springs stained with sleep,
unrelieved trees burdened with apricots.

Here, a man herded ivory sheep
with black mountain dogs; the seals
watched a tractor spin. We too
were once watched by seals. Here, the sheep
gone to wild, the heart of the barn,
the ghost of the bull who died.
The hush of young cedars recruit rebel fields.

Children of the lighthouse, we squatted
at the lipping tide. One by one, pastel godlings,
(what do starfish see?)
we picked a path to the sea wall,
released stone bombs into the fire streaked bay;
something slow about their descent,
something round in the sound,
something so in the fleeting hole,
we dropped them again and again.
The sound might have been a temple gong
if water were bronze.

# SALTSPRING, SEPTEMBER 10, 2001

The need to know how the breeze, the rock
lost in a day
how the arch of a foot placed on a stone breast

the cupped palms of waves
the need to know how
lost in a day
the sea snuffling at sand

how tired waves like dandelions
held too long in a child's hand
the need, lost

of moss without touching
the need to know how
the rose hips on low bushes

how the grey blues
the rose, the rust and jade
how the black dog

swimming away
the need
how the talking crows

how the limp snails
separate from their holds
how the stone

wedged in the fissure
as the tide pulled out
and stopped

# UNNAMED

Waiting on the platform
in the instant of her death
she shed the pain, let go
with a shiver of happiness,
standing by the empty tracks.
An enormous cat filled her arms.

They stood in shadow; across the rails
a northbound sun.
She let go her name, a trace of fog,
a preconception, never hers,
an archway of wild roses. She saw
an unborn daughter, untouchable, sleek
in the light of the other side.

A train arrived, paused.
Names had been mistakes.
She gripped the cat and boarded.
The train was fast and empty,
kissed with ignorance;
thousands of lives in unknown kitchens
blurred by.

The train travels fast,
swallowed by that which has no name.
The cat, warm, grows heavy in her arms.
How can she put it down,
so far away from home?

# IV

# FOURTH WORLD

1.

Will you have a name? Battering
windows, there, grasshopper! against glass,
leaping on a pen-gouged desk, passing
through sun spots and drafts,
then caught, panting in your armor,
fighting until I open my hands,
leaning out the window sill. *Remember
this*, I have time to say, before the black
appears, the hot sound of feather-edge.
Your glass wings crack in its hollow beak
just beyond my reach from the window ledge.
On a curled tongue within its collapsing cheek,
your eye still sees. The crow folds
into a pocket of sky. All is still, and cold.

*2.*

Sweet red beetles hammer the shut windows
and bribe the wind to guide them in
through cracks. One rides my fourth toe like a raft.
They've come in caseloads from Vietnam, shipped
to work the fields without further information.
They can't know about this latitude,
though the way they slam the heated glass,
someone must have told them about snow.
Last week they moved into the guest room.
When the guest came, I put out green towels
and said he'd have to share. But today
they slip in by the hundreds and I must,
I must, vacuum them as fast as they appear.

*3.*

I take the squash bugs, slow as ice,
perched on gilded frames, out to join the others
making Fourth World homes under leaves.
Before this, one or two have wintered here.
I called them Ernest or Methuselah
for their prehistoric joints, forgot them
and discovered them again, said *Hello Ernest*
and went on. Today, they greet me when I wake
and search my folded clothes for winter sleep,
too many now for names. I herd them into jars.
Blind to larger forces, they face the sharp November air,
this morning's frost melted from the field.
They've survived all history without my house:
surely, they know important things.

4.

While I read in bed in sky blue pajamas,
a seven-legged spider lowers to my page,
treks across the opiate drama
Kubla Khan, slipping over ink press reeds unafraid,
threads Xanadu, lifeless oceans, dancing rocks.
Into the canting valley, the spider tests the book,
sounds the depth before she moves—balks
as I shift, thinking a deadly stroke,
the sound my pages make slamming shut.
*Go on, cross the canyon—you're safe*
*enough for now. But soon you should look up.*
Overhead, my new neighbors flagellate
themselves, gaunt and cloudy-haired,
chanting quarter tones and unknown prayers.

# OTHER SINS MORE DEADLY

I wish to be a three-toed sloth,
so on my head when I fall into sleep,
a researcher might place a Petri dish
of water (blessed by every known religion);
to sleep with all assurance that sleeping
is divine; to wake and show
that through the night I'd kept the dish aligned;
to stay ignorant of jungle news;
mirror-eyed, bemused;
to fecundate my silky loves sparingly,
be slow to mate; to live
in the world, disguised as the world,
unnoticed as a stone, and so sprawl
moss-like in a tree, aging inconceivably.

# KILLING THE GOLDFISH

during this, my own disintegration,
"Captain," fantailed, potbellied,
bent in half and bloody with disease,
with a will uncommon in fish bowls,
for weeks, his frantic repeated
dive and stab, unable to eat,
something in his refusal to die,
oh, something in his hunger, the cruelty,
something released in the pop
of the shovel against gold on flagstone,
the small being exploded back
to the atomic god from which it came—

# WINDOWLESS

Fog occupies this room, windowless,
and harbors her silhouette, as if
it's known her longer than memory. Chilled,
she pats the walls she can't see, searches
for the mouth of the draft; wet air pulls blood
from her skin. She is blind; we are blind
(we are what we are,) others here,
arms, breasts, buttocks, skin as cold as hers.
In the mirk just now, her fingers find a pear
on an ancient stem, ragged leaves
in the fog that commands us, soldiers to our nature,
unable to do what we know; forgive us.
If she eats this pear, what then? Eat. Bring us
to our senses, to our lost and beautiful senses.

# SLIDING

Shadows slip down driveways—bears
moaning at night, silver-tipped visions
rocking paw to paw and disappearing
behind stop signs.

All the world is sliding—
rain on green mountainsides, birth canals,
vanishing laps and old age,
those worn wet trails. I too slip
down sluices of wet moss.
There goes the old mill. Sliding.
A row of neat houses, a museum, a parliament.

A blind boy slides beside me on his bedroom door,
equipped with air tanks and rations.
He's seen the omens in sudden clearings.

Here's a yellow grizzly standing broadside
in our way, wet-tufted and musty.
The boy banks by him and vanishes.
I prepare to crash.

Here is a glass door; on the other side
a black bear, dressed in a pin striped suit with waistcoat.
I open a door for him; and as he pads upright
across a marble floor, he tips his bowler hat,
to my relief, for last night I heard the banshees sing,
and I thought they were singing for this world.

# READING SEMIOTICS,
# LATE SEPTEMBER, 2001

I brake countless times for squirrels—
perhaps acorn futures are falling,
the smell of immanent loss.
They run to gather what they can;
I too have errands.

Their dead bodies multiply, while crows
follow asphalt on invisible threads.
Simple deeds are heightened now,
when stable flies leave paddocks
and head upwind into any warm draft,
when beetles look for cracks holding heat.

The fragile are everywhere.
They have lost their trust of days;
dependable hours turn shifty
and blue sky conceals—something.
Yet they continue across the semiotics
of double yellow lines. What else can they do?
They feel their children running in their veins.

Today on the way to buy apples and flour,
I turned my car into this field
in a slow question mark. There is sibilance,
grass against metal. The cows are gone.
The stone walls are still mended,
the field hood-high in goldenrod,
and the seedlings of birch and oak
will be a forest soon. Sitting in fine gold dust
under a September sun, what else can I do?

# BULLS

The bull, horns flashing over sand,
has splintered through the holding fence,
loose again, searching
for the pungent scent of provenance.
Wild cattle on the plains lift their heads to listen.

And somewhere picadors kick ribby geldings,
plant flags in open flesh, while petals
rain from lovers in the stands
who will hold a bloody ear
after the last ceremony. Ask all the mothers
if this was what they wanted for their sons.

The long days are done.
Oceans clash, tangled white-capped horns,
bulls and men blacken under flame-lit skies,
and through outlasting clouds
hawks free-fall in each other's talons.
The sky, excited, drops the earth
from its long embrace, as homeless
cowbirds fly above the sinking range.
It was delicate, when it was.

# THE LAST FLIGHT

In a coastal cave streaked with rose
and ash, just safe
above the white-capped lanes
we watch the long tailed phoenix fly
so determined, so immense
that were there sun
the day would darken more
so near, we hear the whip of wings
the whistle of its tail—a feathered river jeweled
with tangled wires and hooks
and after, only wave
after wave—

# READING THE NEWS

It's finally possible to microwave
the perfect egg. I take a shallow bowl
with Mandarin carp hand-painted on the bottom,
puncture the yolk, before
my daughters wake, before the peace
of night is gone, sip tea in raku
placed on teak beneath a spray of roses.
The crossword in the paper begs eight letters
for what of innocence is drowned.
I find comfort in the news as being far away.
A helicopter skims by rooftops.
Under beating blades young gods
drop shards of paper into air, a test of wind,
a non-parade. One takes Polaroids
of geraniums blown off balconies.
Now more helicopters come,
ordered bees from unforgiving hives.
I wake the children. Take them to the cellar.
Musicians rush in from the street,
and school girls from upstairs arrive half-dressed
as bombs start falling to the east. The air
grows strange with scents of strawberries
and solvent; the cockatiel drops noiseless

from its perch with tightened wings.
From a tiny window I see
a yellow dog lying in the road.
Now we pant in the juleped air.
In sun, the spring leaves fall, a snow
of pale green. Fine powder dusts
the windshields of the silent cars.
My eyes begin to bleed.
It's morning, don't ask where,
as if it's someplace else.

# THE MAN IN A BOW TIE,
## LATE WINTER, BELIZE

Bow-tie dangling, thinking of owl chicks
warmed by snow-dusted mothers back home,
he laughs at the moon in the shark blue sky,
a yellow dog smiling too, everybody laughing,
as palm fronds rip like pirate flags,
his bare feet on the sandy road. Nearby
a magpie sirens, clicks and whirrs
like his lens shutter. The smooth-skinned girl,
gold-chained, cuts a cabbage. He watches
the head swing up and down on the blade.
The dog slinks around soft tires
and unseen monkeys howl.
The cabbage sails up and down,
knife in its heart too tired to withdraw,
and he laughs. *Careful with that ax, Eugene.*
No one responds. No one speaks English.
The flour-dusted mother rests her large breasts
on the counter as he asks with his hands
for five cigarettes from a fresh pack,
like the workmen who command
the girl's loud nails to pick cellophane.
They leave their machetes outside.

He asks for four eggs, no, yes. He must have
three Oreos, testing what the girl might sell.
Failing again to find any eyes, he holds out coins
to be counted, then leaves as unnoticed as the dog,
not forgetting to nod at the moon and sun
as he searches his pockets for a room key,
but his cabbaged heart doesn't feel like humming.

# DAY BREAK

Before dawn, she presses her palms against the day.
Corridors open and close, guarded by gibbons
who threaten her calves with gold-carved teeth.
Priests in loosened collars occupy her house,
drunk on grasshoppers. She asks them to leave
but it is she who leaves. Then struggles to sink back.
Why? It's the real world that she loves.
Soon she'll shake hours like wrapped packages,
holding each up to the light, but here
she reaches for the lost, familiar whole,
where nothing is untrue, plots unclouded
by discomforts of living, non sequitur unquestioned.
She denies dawn, this rain, this waking green.
in the shakeable hours, she will end,
the way a pine tree ends in a thousand needles.
She shifts her face into the flannel gag
of pillow, but the pale-eyed weight
of world-loving presses with insistence.

V

# IF WISHES WERE LIONS

In the wild they relish hot blood, scavenge cold,
and lick until the spills come clean,
but caged, contoured like the treeless land,
this one yawns with missing teeth.
Sand rises cone-shaped in its bowl. The hours gnaw
at its sharp hips, limp phallus, the caves that were its eyes.
It listens to the soldiers eat the caged deer.
It hears the yellow bear go crazy, and the elephant shot.
Mortars shatter the aquarium and the water
turns to dust, while the dusty wild boar goes untouched.
Dark with age, it snuffles cartons, tossed into its cage,
fragrant with tobacco crumbs of vanished cigarettes.
Officers jab and turn their backs. The keeper begs for food.
Steal the keys! Open the cage so it can clean the streets
of both bloods, hot and cold. Its throat wider than the treeless hills,
let it walk the emptied alleys and lie on creeping light
in some stone corner with its bellyful of fists, on and on.

## ELECTION

There is a panic in the fall. Everyone
becomes a parent whose baby crawls naked
on a cold day across an eight lane interstate.
It doesn't matter if we pedal to work,
or hunt wolves from low flying planes;
it doesn't matter if we argued with our son
when he joined the Air Force and keep
his last letter in the Bible we disavowed,
or if we think that God is on our side.
The world spins, and it belongs
to others with cell phones driving fast.
Late from your commute, you enter
our curtained kitchen with cheddar
and bread, the brandy to stew the peaches.
As you put the bag on the counter,
bears swim in the open sea for an ice shelf
that has moved four hundred miles away.

# NECESSARY ANGELS

Oh Holy Night
The stars are brightly shining
On what so proudly we hail

Sweet hay slips from the crèche
The burro, a poor man's Pegasus
The baby born as strangely as Dionysus
From Zeus's thigh. Hear the angel voices!

O Zeus, O Yahweh, O Jesus, O Allah
We have run through you all
Led by the light of faith serenely
The foe, dread silence

A children's choir, fingers steepled
(All kneel)
The sleeve of my neighbor touching mine
(All stand)

The thrill of hope, the weary world rejoices
Sings good will towards men
And the bombs bursting in air
And if I were a shepherd I would bring a lamb
If I were a parent, would I bring a child?
I've stopped singing. I can't sing along.

## "WHEN THE AKKADIAN EMPIRE COLLAPSED, 2200 B.C., EVEN THE EARTHWORMS DIED"

*——from The New Yorker*

You know the show well.
You watch the spotlights search
the empty chairs for elephants,
great red drums the ringmaster skirts
with his whip, the giants waiting
limp in the wings, ferrets snaking
through children and parents,
sleek among distracted feet, into pockets,
stealing thoughts for fading gypsies
to read. The clown on his tricycle
travels in smaller and smaller circles;
the flowers in his hat are trying to spell.
How many days has the rain fallen?
Has the wind called for your bare arms?
I wish I could unplug you, hand you a shovel,
and have you turn the dark soil,
witness the sincerity of bloodworms.
Can we turn off the lights?
Re-learn darkness?

# PSALM

Ringing bone on bone, distant
undertones in the ear, restless
antiphonal choruses, bones
sucked of marrow, used as weapons,
crushed to fern dust which bleeds
in rain-washed fugal drips
on the heads of ant lions.
Listen. Motives recapitulate.
Hear them, hidden in the glitter of leaves,
thinning, less varied than imagined—
portents and passions, and quick asides
trying to lighten shell-shocked moments,
the way a pack mule shakes
its sweating hide under harness.
Sing the psalm of your enemy.
He too becomes dull, listening to the sounds
of the late meal ending, has lost a child,
and watches, weighted with counterpoint,
the powder of bone settle like salt
on half-grown crops.

# FLOOD

The trout flipped her tail and scraped a tree.

She squirmed through schools of daffodils
        and rooms of dancing chairs,
through swarms of clattering aspirin jars
        and sinking clouds of sheep.
        She laid her eggs in robins' nests.

Some days the river is like this.

# ELEGY FOR SILENCE

Painters used to need pristine planes
to mark what came—inner / outer
orders flashing off each other,
linen gessoed so, stretched to argue
with the brush, the right tooth for biting back.
And cellos needed quiet
that would stretch to hold lines taut,
so nothing interfered, the way the dog
itching by the bed, ruined sex, though
we laughed and said it didn't matter.
It's over. Track up the museum floor
in paint-dipped shoes, stack your amps and wail.

# CHROMATIC SCALE

Black Steinway, Model A, 1927;
Coffee-ringed; where passing hours
      Carve shadows;
Delivered shining—now children
      Draw sun and trees in
Each month's dust. Your keys raised clouds in
French West Africa, tusks, careful with newborn,
      Fondled still wet hides,
Grave heart. Now you are cold
      Geometry.  Your soundboard stood
And listened spruce-eared to
      Assonant rain. Your frame slept underground,
Became molten, manufactured. Now your pins,
Carbon steel, loosen like old teeth.  In
      Cross-strung caverns, echoes
Distend—rain and wind
      Decay off chords like squalls in seashells.
Easing into keys until they yield like
Flesh—I decay too,
      Following you to abstract
Gardens, wanting what
      God knew before the names of things.
As you pass through me into the open
      Anima, where Lisztian sparrows dodge, lions
Bellow and naked human voices

Call—the hubris of Germany never
  Capsized, willowy sex from Brazil—all of this
Drinkable—the self
  Drains away. I believe. I believe
Everything you say. Pianos do not lie.

# FICTION

Beginning with *THE END*—is she,
to whom I am attached, forged line by printed line,
after her emptied champagne glass has been taken
from the table, after the closing kiss, is she,
whom I have come to know more intimately
than myself, who sleeps now on cool cotton,
child-like on the first night of happily ever after,
the sky filled with wafers of unserious snow,
is she, who has been guiltless, proud, humiliated
and justified, who has longed as I have longed,
and is leaving now, wealth assured, for a palace
and a white sand beach, will the sand
not have sand fleas, and the palace plumbing
never need adjustment? Will the tiny balsa stretchers
of her parasol never snap? In this pause
on the last blank page, is she to be forever
content, without change? Yes, please, yes.

# CULTURAL DISOBEDIENCE

You say the peony is slipped, a prostitute
showing everything. Dandelions,
twenty children each, crowd the backyard projects —
fuck, it's a trend, soggy bits of paper too demoralized to fly,
the tough biology of a cigarette butt.
In the cutting bed you see the rose blight,
and beetles gnawing like hyenas on the infant
copper beech, a tiny mouse head left
on a pike of grass—trailing a bit of esophagus.
Violence is the ready art.
But wild tongues of iris offset your troubled rose.
Here, an albino spider stops again on paper-whites;
the hornet comes from perfect circles in the ground.
Now, when petals are acts of cultural disobedience,
love each dusk and dawn. Spin dervishly.
At this late date the stars continue above the fields
and we could, if we chose,
be grass-soaked under a midnight husband.
Beauty is uncontrollable.


*after Dave Hickey*

# POSTLUDE

And so they asked:

*What is the moon like?*
And the poet said a half-baked cookie, not very round.
A Brownie baked that moon for her first badge,
and that's why it's yellow, caught in the tree.

*What's the tree like?*
Trees are stubble on an earthy chin.
Arboretums make strange beards.
I tramped through trees
in my spiked heels and the soil itched.

*What are your shoes like?*
My shoes? My shoes are smug smiles,
returned from Arabian Nights.
When no one was looking, I took them off
and crossed the gold stalls barefoot,
my toes naked near the painted hooves.

*What is your nose like?*
My toes, you mean.

*Your nose, we mean.*
My nose. My nose is a sidewalk
which once was a cow path.
My nose is a typewriter, obsolete.
My nose is a tired nun
once capable of ecstasy.
Every day my sense of smell fades,
like a goldfish kept in town water.

*What are goldfish like?*
And then the poet said:
After all this time
what can be said that hasn't been said
to answer your endless ache?
Decide what goldfish are like for yourself.

# BLUEBOTTLE

*after Pablo Neruda*

The fly trapped inside this poem
pads the walls with sticky steps, wings
as sharp as tongues, fussing at the routine
line breaks of his dry aquarium.
His eyes blur the curves of words,
he counts the feet, ignores the rhyme (which makes
him larger than he is at times,) and tastes
the tasteless consonance and swerves
from deconstruction.
                              Upside down and startled
by the echo of a rusty voice,
he hears a melody he used to sing.
He tries to wash it from his head,
wishing for a speck of bliss;
something visceral, literal, and green.

# BACH

He lies in dingy sheets
and touches her, while trucks below
shift gears and pigeons shuffle on the roof,
the building lit with midnight news,
her piano on the fourteenth floor,
and all her scores stacked high.
From her open window, night snow
drifts on piano wires.
He sits on the black bench, ghost
that he is, hands on hers as she plays.
A neighbor shoulders through the stacks
to demand she omit the parts with
all those notes. One by one,
windows blink and shutter.
It's nothing, he says.
Nothing.
Play on.

# ACKNOWLEDGEMENTS

Some of these poems have been published as a chapbook, *Fourth World* (Adastra, 2010).

Some have appeared, sometimes in slightly different form or under different titles, in the following publications:

*Berkshire Review*: "Denying Archeology," "Other Sins More Deadly"

*Coe Review:* "Reading The News"

*Comstock Review*: "Living Treasure, Japanese Cup"

*Confrontation*: "Bluebottle Sonnet"

*Connecticut River Review*: "Decoy," "Reading Semiotics," Late September, 2001"

*descant:* "Free Radical"

*Epicenter:* "Raven," "Research"

*Equinox:* "About Lying"

*Hear a Poet, There a Poet:* from "Fourth World"

*The Best of Lady Churchill's Rosebud Wristlet*, "Sliding"

*Limestone,* from "Fourth World"

*MacGuffin:* "Against The Bit"

*Massachusetts Cultural Council, online:* "Potato Cannon," "Horses Are Not Predators"

*New England Watershed:* "Flood"

*New Millennium Writings:* "Cello in Apartment 2B," "Stalls"

*Nimrod:* "Cultural Disobedience," "Different Gold Than Gilt"

*Northwest Review:* "Last Rites"

*Poetry Daily:* "Raven"

*Portland Review:* "Bach," "Guest"

*South Carolina Review:* "Bulls"

*Weber Studies:* "Perfect Pitch," "Saltspring"

*Westview:* "Last Flight"

# AUTHOR

D M Gordon's poems and stories have been published widely. Prizes include The Betsy Colquitt Award from *descant*, The Editor's Choice Award from the *Beacon Street Review*, and first prize from *Glimmer Train*. Phi Beta Kappa, Masters in Music from Boston University, she's the recipient of a 2008 Massachusetts Cultural Council Artist Fellowship in fiction, having been a finalist in poetry in 2004. She currently works as an editor and facilitates a weekly public discussion of contemporary poetry for Forbes Library in Northampton, Massachusetts. She is the author of *Fourth World* (Adastra Press, 2010) and is at work on a novel set in the Gulf Islands.

*Nightly, at the Institute of the Possible*
was designed and printed by Steve Strimer
for Hedgerow Books of Levellers Press

The cover art is "Voix du Sang" by René Magritte

The paper is Mohawk Vellum
The type is Fournier